Family La

A Guide To
Child Custody
In New Jersey

2nd Edition

Bari Zell Weinberger, Esq.

FAMILY LAW REFERENCE COLLECTION
Weinberger Divorce & Family Law Group

A Guide To Child Custody In New Jersey

Table of Contents

About The Author

Bari Z. Weinberger, Esq. is a certified matrimonial law attorney and founding partner of Weinberger Divorce & Family Law Group of New Jersey. Ms. Weinberger has been named a *Top Women in Law* by New Jersey Law Journal and carries an AV Preeminent (highest) peer rating from Martindale Hubbelll. She recently celebrated 10 years of recognition on the state's SuperLawyers list.

In addition to working with clients at her firm, Weinberger Divorce & Family Law Group, Ms. Weinberger is the Associate Author of the New Jersey Family Law Practice, 15th Ed., a 5-volume treatise utilized by virtually every family law judge and practitioner in the State of New Jersey.

www.WeinbergerLawGroup.com

Disclaimer

This book provides a general overview of New Jersey divorce and family law matters for informational purposes only. The contents included do not in any way supplement or replace legal advice obtained by a qualified and licensed attorney.

The information provided herein is based solely upon my professional experiences in the areas of New Jersey divorce and family law. While every effort has been made to ensure that the information contained in this book is helpful and of high quality, no representations or warranties of any kind are made with regard to the completeness or accuracy of the included content.

Please note that information provided within this guide is current as of publication date. Due to the complexity and frequency with which the divorce and family laws change, you should consult with a qualified attorney to determine the best course of action for your specific legal needs.

If you require legal advice based on the specifics of your case as it relates to New Jersey laws, please feel free to reach out to our office to schedule a consultation with one of our experienced attorneys. It would be our pleasure to help you.

For more information about other topics related to family law, such as alimony, domestic violence, prenuptial agreements, family mediation, child support, domestic partnerships, or any other family law related topics, please ask us about our other books. All guides in the series are designed, like this one, to help you to make sound decisions regarding your family's individual situation. Please keep in mind, however, that these books contain general information, and not legal advice. Always direct specific questions about your own situation to an attorney.

Weinberger Divorce & Family Law Group
Safeguarding Your Future™

Letter from the Author

As a parent, as someone who witnessed divorce as a child, and as a family law attorney who has worked with countless clients over the years, I know that child custody is often the most pressing issue that must be resolved when parents decide to separate or divorce, and also the most contentious.

Right now, it may be extremely painful for you to contemplate losing any time with your kids, or you may feel like your spouse is waging a war to alienate you from your children. Out of anger and resentment, one of you may have already demanded sole custody, without stopping to consider what this legal maneuver truly means for your family's future.

There is little doubt about it, the issues surrounding child custody cases can be complicated – both legally and emotionally. How do you know which custody arrangement, whether sole, joint, or shared, is right for your children? How do you see beyond your own hurt to make healthy decisions for your family? And how do you change unfair child custody and parenting time decisions that may have been made in the past?

As you begin the process of arranging child custody, one of the best things you can do is arm yourself with thorough, up-to-date information about family law in New Jersey. This is the reason why I have put together this book. We are a law firm dedicated solely to the practice of family law. This guide was created based on countless years of hands-on experience with real families, just like yours, who have struggled with and overcome legal obstacles related to their child custody issues.

My hope is that after reading the following pages, you are able to work out a parenting arrangement that provides your children with the opportunity to grow and thrive. However, because each child custody matter is unique, a book like this can only go so far in guiding you through the process. While I have made every effort to address common scenarios that you might encounter, the information presented here is intended neither as individual advice nor as a substitute for legal representation. Like any other area of law, family law is subject to frequent change and endless variations, depending on the details of your specific circumstances.

This is why I feel so strongly that the assistance of a qualified family law attorney is essential when dealing with children's issues. Please know that I have carefully handpicked my team of family lawyers at Weinberger Divorce & Family Law Group to ensure that we offer the highest standard of representation in child custody matters. No matter which of our attorneys you may decide to work with, you and your family can feel rest assured that you will be treated with the same level of outstanding care and attention.

I can personally attest that at Weinberger Divorce & Family Law Group, we truly understand what you are going through. If you are in need of legal assistance in your child custody matter, please do not hesitate to reach out to us for a free consultation.

We're here to help, always.

All my best,
Bari Z. Weinberger, Esq.

Chapter 1

Child Custody and
Separation / Divorce

Informing children about a change in marital status and talking to them about how their lives will change as a result are often the most difficult aspects of separation or divorce for parents.

While it is important to acknowledge that parental separation and divorce may be very hard on children, parents can take comfort in knowing that the distress is temporary, provided of course that both parents are able to come together and co-parent in a civilized manner for the sake of their children.

When parents are unable to set aside feelings of personal bitterness, or stress from the financial concerns that divorce so frequently entails, we know that children often continue to feel unsettled and confused, sometimes for extended periods of time. However, when both parents make a concerted effort to move beyond the difficulties between them and work to form two new, separate but coordinated family systems, children can regain their equilibrium much more quickly. As hard as it may be to believe right now, some children even eventually grow to view the divorce as a positive change in their family's structure.

If you are a parent facing impending separation or divorce, make a plan with your children's other parent to tell them about the decision together, and be sure to give each child ample opportunity to ask questions. Make an effort to assure your children that the bond between a parent and child is different than the couple bond and cannot be broken through divorce. Let them know that they will still have two parents who love them and will be involved in their lives to the maximum extent possible.

This book can help you plan in advance and make informed decisions regarding common legal problems that arise between unmarried or divorcing parents. It will guide you as you attempt to work out parenting arrangements that provide your children with ample opportunities to grow and thrive.

" Parents are free to make their own arrangements about parenting time, provided that a parenting schedule does not compromise the child's best interests. "

Bari Z. Weinberger, Esq.

How Courts Determine Custody

Agreements between Parents

For the most part, parents are free to make their own agreements about how to share parental responsibilities and parenting time, provided that a parenting schedule does not compromise what are considered the child's best interests. This presents an opportunity for parents to work together to develop a schedule that will work for everyone in the restructured family.

Except in cases with extenuating circumstances such as domestic violence, parents in New Jersey who have disputes about child custody or parenting time are required to participate in no-cost confidential mediation soon after the commencement of their case. Parents attend these sessions without attorneys, and a court-appointed mediator attempts to assist them in reaching a mutual agreement on custody and parenting. Agreements reached during mediation are non-binding until they are executed as a formal agreement.

In cases where the parents have a high degree of conflict, the court may also appoint an attorney to represent the child's interests, or a special fact-finder called a "guardian ad litem" to investigate circumstances affecting the child and make a report to the court. In some cases, psychological evaluation of a parent or child may be necessary. The parents usually must pay the costs associated with any such services.

As a general rule, parents are better off determining their own parenting and custody arrangements. Judges seldom have the time or intricate knowledge about an individual family to be able to make such a personal decision. Involving a guardian ad litem or custody evaluator can be extremely expensive and time-consuming, and only rarely do these measures result in significant improvement over what the parents might have been able to agree upon initially. Nevertheless, where parents cannot agree on an acceptable plan, the court will ultimately make the decision for them.

You can find statutes dealing with children and parents in Title 9 of the New Jersey Statutes Annotated (N.J.S.A.), which is available in searchable unannotated form online from the New Jersey Legislature. The statute concerning forms of child custody in New Jersey is N.J.S.A. 9:2-4. Several other chapters in Title 9 affect decisions and agreements regarding child custody.

Factors Affecting Custody Determinations

Courts base custody decisions on the best interests of the children involved. This means that a child's physical and emotional welfare are the primary considerations in any custody determination. While courts assess each situation individually, the law in New Jersey instructs judges to begin by assuming that children will benefit from maintaining frequent and continuing contact with both of their parents and from having both parents share the rights and responsibilities of raising children.

New Jersey law provides courts with additional guidance by listing some of the specific factors that a judge should consider in making a decision about what is in a child's best interest. The listed factors are:

- the parents' ability to agree, communicate and cooperate in matters relating to the child,

- the parents' willingness to accept custody and any history of unwillingness to allow parenting time not based on substantiated abuse,
- the interaction and relationship of the child with parents and siblings,
- any history of domestic violence,
- the safety of the child and either parent from physical abuse by the other parent,
- the preference of a child who is of sufficient age and capacity to reason so as to form an intelligent decision,
- the child's needs,
- the stability of the home environment offered,
- the quality and continuity of the child's education,
- the parent's fitness,
- the geographical proximity of the parents' homes,
- the extent and quality of the time spent with the child prior to or subsequent to the separation,
- each parents' employment responsibilities, and
- the age and number of the children.
(N.J.S.A. 9:2-4.)

This list is not exclusive. Courts are free to consider any factor that could impact the best interests of a child. The following is a more detailed explanation of some of the factors a judge may consider in making a custody decision:

Physical Health and Safety

A child's physical safety is always a primary concern. In awarding custody, judges strive to ensure that neither parent poses any risk of physical violence either to the child or to the child's other parent. A judge may limit parenting time to supervised visitation if a parent's behavior, due to a history of domestic violence or other circumstances, appears to pose a substantial risk of harm to the child. In extreme circumstances a judge may even disallow visitation entirely. In most cases, however, a court will find that it is in the child's best interests to have some contact with each parent. We include information later in this chapter detailing the types of circumstances that might lead a court to impose limitations on custody and visitation.

Social and Emotional Needs

In assessing a child's social and emotional needs, judges consider the general stability of the environment in each parent's home, as well as the quality of the interaction between the child and each parent. The extent to which each parent participated in child care both before and since the separation is also important, as this establishes both the parent's commitment to assuming responsibilities of child care and the probable strength of the parent-child bond. Courts also consider sibling relationships to be very important and will usually try very hard to keep siblings together.

Practical Tip: When possible, take advantage of therapy and support groups for children.
Almost all children who are going through or have gone through their parents' divorce will benefit from outside support. Sometimes children blame themselves, or harbor anger against one or both parents. With divorce being so commonplace today, there is no reason for any child to feel alone with these kinds of feelings. Participating in therapy or special support groups for children of families going through divorce can help children heal emotionally.

The Child's Own Preferences

A judge who believes that a child is old enough and mature enough to provide intelligent input into the custody decision may allow the child to state a preference. The law does not specify a minimum age, but the older and more emotionally mature a child is, the better the argument that the child should have substantial input. The child's preference will never be more than one factor in determining best interests, but a judge might weigh the preference more or less heavily depending on all the other circumstances.

In some cases, children will voice an opinion without being asked. If this does not happen, parents would be wise to exercise great caution before asking a child to reveal an opinion. It is very difficult for a child to express a wish to live with one parent without experiencing feelings of betrayal toward the other parent. Judges generally question children about such matters only in chambers rather than in open court.

In a highly contested case in which the court has appointed a guardian ad litem, the guardian ad litem may interview the child, the parents, and any third parties who have pertinent information about the child's situation. These could include teachers, school counselors, therapists, pediatricians, and grandparents or other close relatives. The guardian ad litem then submits a comprehensive report to the court with a recommendation regarding custody and parenting.

The use of a guardian ad litem can help to protect children in a custody dispute, as it allows a child to share an opinion in confidence as one aspect of an overall investigation. Parents should strive to resolve custody and visitation matters without forcing a child to feel placed in the middle and under no circumstances should a parent ever make a child feel guilty for having expressed a preference.

The Parents' Co-parenting and Communication Skills

A court will consider each parent's ability to communicate and cooperate with the other parent. The key factor is the ability to co-parent in a peaceful and civilized manner. Willingness to be actively involved in a child's life is important, but a parent must also be careful not to interfere with the child's time with the other parent. In a situation where both parents desire primary custody but one parent is also expressing an unfounded desire to prevent the children from having significant contact with the other parent, the parent who is more willing to allow frequent and continuing contact is likely to have the advantage. Courts are especially careful to consider co-parenting abilities before ordering arrangements that require both parents to share legal and physical custody, because these arrangements require parents to work closely with each other.

Parental Fitness

Although the law states that a court should consider a parent's "fitness," it also states that a parent should not be considered "unfit" unless the parent's conduct has a substantial adverse effect on the child. Parents who have unresolved anger toward a former partner sometimes wish to raise every aspect of the ex-partner's personality that a judge might possibly interpret in a negative way. This can lead to an unnecessary and unproductive escalation of conflict, and often results only in making the complaining parent appear petty and vindictive. Before raising parental misconduct as an indicator of unfitness, be sure to consider carefully how the conduct is likely to affect the child. If it is unlikely to have any negative effect, you may be wise to let it go.

Practical Considerations

Practical considerations that may affect a custody arrangement include the distance between the parents' homes, the location of a child's school, parents' respective employment responsibilities, and the number and ages of any other children in each home. Courts do not have a magic formula telling them how to weigh such matters. A factor one judge considers to be important may seem to be of minimal importance to another judge. If there are practical factors involved in your case, be sure that the court understands their potential impact.

Practical Tip: Take parenting classes seriously.
In some states, including New Jersey, couples who have issues regarding custody, parenting time, or child support must attend parenting education programs, unless they are excused due to a mitigating circumstance such as domestic violence. In the New Jersey class for divorcing parents, a family law mediator and typically two social workers present information about effects of divorce on children and children's needs during and after the divorce. Each parent attends the class separately. If the court directs you to attend any kind of parenting class, make sure that you go. The court will consider any failure to attend required programs when making custody and visitation decisions.

Chapter 2

Available Options in New Jersey
Child Custody

Although many parents are accustomed to thinking about custody as limited to either "sole" or "joint," there are actually many different combinations and possibilities in custody arrangements. There are two major components to any parenting plan: physical custody and legal custody.

Physical Custody

Physical custody refers to a child's physical presence with a parent. Depending on how physical custody is defined in a court order or parenting agreement, one or the other parent will also have physical custody during the time that a child is in school or is engaging in regular extracurricular activities. In New Jersey, the term "sole physical custody" refers to a traditional type of parenting arrangement where a child lives with a "custodial parent" the majority of the time. The "non-custodial parent" has visitation time that is generally less than the equivalent of two overnight periods per week, not including vacation and holiday time. Parents with this kind of traditional schedule usually use the "Sole Parenting Worksheet" to calculate child support.

The terms "shared physical custody" or "shared parenting time" generally refer to arrangements where a child spends the equivalent of more than two overnight periods per week with each parent. This includes schedules where children alternate blocks of time with each parent, such as three days with one parent and four with the other, or one week at a time with each parent. Parents with these more equal parenting schedules may use the "Shared Parenting Worksheet" to calculate child support. This worksheet refers to the parents as the "Parent of Primary Residence" (PPR) and the "Parent of Alternate Residence" (PAR).

The trend in New Jersey is to apply these newer parenting designations of PPR and PAR to all parents who are co-parenting in separate households, even those with more limited visitation time, and to use the term "parenting time" to refer to all periods of visitation. The philosophy behind this trend recognizes that all parents should be actively involved in parenting, and no parent should be seen as simply "visiting" with a child.

Legal Custody

Legal custody refers to a parent's authority to participate in major decisions regarding a child's health, education, and general welfare. This includes such things as where a child will attend school, what kind of religious upbringing a child will have, and when a child requires medical treatment beyond routine care or emergency treatment. If one parent is awarded sole legal custody, that parent has the authority to make all such major decisions on the child's behalf without consulting the other parent. In joint legal custody, both parents must be involved in the decision making process.

Parents can also share legal custody by assigning some major decisions to one parent and some to the other. For example, an agreement could provide that one parent has the final say in educational decisions and the other in religious decisions, but that both must agree on major medical decisions. While this is a more unusual arrangement, it can sometimes be a good solution and can break a stalemate between parents on how best to divide legal custody.

Combining Custody Options in Parenting Plans: Common Arrangements

Beyond the policy in favor of shared parental responsibility and frequent contact with both parents, New Jersey law does not favor any particular custody arrangement. Courts have authority to divide physical and legal custody between parents in any combination. The following are the most common types of arrangements:

Joint Legal Custody with a Traditional Parenting Schedule:

This type of arrangement is very common and is often acceptable to both parents as it allows both of them to participate actively in their children's lives. Both parents have decision-making authority for the children's major health, education and general welfare issues, while the parent who is with a child at any given time makes day-to-day decisions in the child's best interests and notifies the other parent as appropriate.

In most joint legal custody arrangements, the child resides with one parent the majority of the time—generally more than five days or five overnights in an average week, not including vacation time—and the other parent has a more traditional visitation schedule. The child usually spends alternate weekends with the non-custodial parent (or parent of alternate residence). Parents who live fairly close together often add a mid-week dinner or other mid-week activity for the child and the non-custodial parent.

Shared Legal and Physical Custody:

When parenting time is equal or close to equal for each parent, the parents are generally considered to have shared legal and physical custody. This is a less common arrangement, as it requires a high degree of communication and coordinated co-parenting; only a relatively small percentage of unmarried or divorced parents are capable of achieving and maintaining the required degree of cooperation over time.

Nevertheless, many parents desire a close to equal division of parenting time, and creative scheduling options can often make this work. Some families choose to have children alternate weeks with each parent; others have them spend four days and nights per week with one parent, and three days and nights per week with the other—sometimes alternating the fourth day and night of each week to equalize the time.

Even when the parents have equal or nearly equal time-sharing, they will generally still designate one parent as the PPR and the other as the PAR. The address of the PPR is used as the default address for determining a child's legal residence for school attendance.

There is no bright line distinguishing true shared legal and physical custody from other types of joint legal custody, but the distinction may be important for several different reasons. For example, in a child support case, a court is not likely to make an adjustment for "controlled expenses" (expenses for items a court usually assumes only the PPR will purchase, such as clothing, personal care products or services, and most entertainment and miscellaneous items) unless time-sharing is truly equal.

The distinction between joint custody with a custodial parent or a PPR and fully shared custody was, until recently, also very important in relocation cases. Custodial parents used to have a clear advantage. A parent with shared custody needed to ask the court for a change to primary physical custody before the court could even consider the removal issue. The law on move-away cases changed in 2017, however, with the case of *Bisbing v. Bisbing*. This issue is discussed in depth later in this chapter.

Sole Legal and Physical Custody:

In this type of custody arrangement, the parent who is the residential custodian for the child is also responsible for all major decisions regarding the child's health, education, and welfare, as well as all day-to-day decisions.

The custodial parent is not required to consult with or notify the non-custodial parent. A few parents will agree on this type of arrangement for personal reasons, but in the majority of cases it is an arrangement instituted by a court after a judge has determined that one parent is absent or unfit due to a history of child abuse or neglect, drug addiction, or a similar issue. In the majority of such cases the non-custodial parent will still have visitation with the child, but visitation will often be supervised or restricted to ensure the child's safety.

" Child custody is not limited to either *sole* or *joint*...there are actually many different combinations and possibilities in custody arrangements. **"**

Bari Z. Weinberger, Esq.

Parenting Plan FAQ

What should you include in your parenting plan?

Parenting plans in most states, including New Jersey, must designate the child's primary residence and must indicate how parents will share decision-making on major issues such as education, medical and dental treatment, and religious upbringing. Other specific requirements vary from state to state, but the plan should always include a specific schedule addressing how you and your children's other parent will share time. It is especially important to specify how you will divide holidays, birthdays, and vacations. There is no rule dictating how you must do this. Some parents alternate holidays, but others who live close to one another may divide up time on the actual day. In addition to spelling these details out, you may also want to address the following:

- access to children's medical records, report cards teachers, etc.,
- whether you wish to give each other "first rights of refusal," i.e., the option of stepping in during the other parent's time when the latter is unavailable for a designated number of hours, before the other parent can hire a babysitter or call another relative,
- who will be responsible for specific expenses and how you will share unanticipated expenses,
- who will be responsible for transportation of children and transportation costs,
- who will take off work if necessary to care for a sick child,
- how you will address potential schedule changes or modification of the plan as children get older,

- whether you agree to attend mediation to resolve conflicts over the plan or joint decisions in the future, and
- any other agreements you wish to include.

How specific should your plan be?

Consider various scenarios: If your plan states, for example, that parents will alternate weekends, and one of you refuses to make a child available on the other parent's weekend, can you call the police and ask for enforcement? You can try, but you probably will not succeed in getting immediate help, because there is nothing in this plan that would let a police officer know with any certainty which parent actually has parenting rights on any particular weekend. By contrast, plans that specify time down to the last detail are relatively easy to enforce. Such plans also include less flexibility, but parents are always free to consent to changes.

If you and your child's other parent have difficulty cooperating with one another, you may need to have a schedule that precisely details when a child is to be with each parent, both during the week and during all holiday and vacation periods. On the other hand, if you cannot really conceive of having to resort to law enforcement for help with your parenting schedule, you might be successful with a looser plan. Some parents detail specific time for holidays and vacation periods only, while specifying that the parents will divide time in a certain percentage during a normal week. They agree between themselves how this will usually work, but do not set it in stone by including it in the parenting plan. If you have questions about how specific your plan needs to be, talk to an attorney.

Practical Tip: Keep good records of everything relating to your parenting plan.

Unless you have a court order declaring that you are your child's sole legal custodian, be sure to keep the other parent fully informed of all important events or changes to the parenting schedule, as well as any medical, extracurricular, or similar issues affecting your child. Document all communications. If you need to go back to court in the future, proof of such communications can be the key to obtaining the result you are seeking or defeating a result the other parent is seeking that would be contrary to your interests. Programs such as Family Wizard, available from the Our Family Wizard website: http://bit.ly/family-wizard, are an excellent resource for maintaining a joint family calendar and documenting important events. An ordinary diary is also a good tool for daily tracking. If the other parent has chronic problems complying with the schedule (lateness, frequent cancellations, or not getting a child to school or extracurricular activities regularly and on time) the written record will show the court exactly what happened and when.

Chapter 3

Finding the Best Custody Option

Many parents are able to work together successfully to come up with a custody and visitation plan that addresses the best interests of the children and fits the schedules and preferences of both parents. Others must go through a fair amount of juggling and negotiation to develop a plan; neither parent may be completely satisfied with the final result, but they have a plan that is workable and meets the children's needs. Still other parents will have a difficult time agreeing on a plan even after extensive negotiation and mediation.

If you and your child's other parent are having difficulty agreeing on a plan, you may need to consult with a family law attorney to get a better idea of what a judge might decide in your case. Whatever your plan eventually looks like, it should take into account all the practical considerations facing your family, such as work schedules, children's school requirements and activities, planned travel, child care needs, location and involvement of extended family members, different ages of children, planning for future changes, and any other situation that affects your family members.

Is There Really a "Best" Option?

Parents often wonder what kind of plan is the overall best option for children. Unfortunately, there is no simple answer to this question. If there was, many disagreements between separating parents could surely be avoided, as the great majority of parents truly want to do whatever will help their children to thrive.

While experts agree that, except in very unusual circumstances, a child will benefit from the involvement of both parents, there is little agreement on exactly what this means. There is no such thing as an ideal solution; drawbacks exist both with traditional parenting arrangements and with more contemporary arrangements that lean toward equal time-sharing. The following are some things you may want to consider in developing a parenting plan:

Traditional Parenting Plans:

The primary risk with a more traditional arrangement, where children's time with a non-custodial parent is generally limited to alternate weekends and an occasional mid-week activity, is that the non-custodial parent may be less involved in routine parenting activities and may function more like a babysitter or a peripheral relative than a parent. Another potentially serious drawback is that the parent who takes on or continues in the role of primary caretaker may be limited to employment options that provide the flexibility required for the parent to give priority to children's needs—and this sometimes means lower paying employment options.

Equal-Time Parenting Plans:

Parents need to reside in close proximity to one another and have a civil co-parenting relationship for successful implementation of this kind of shared parenting arrangement. With equal or nearly equal parenting time, there is generally a tremendous amount of back and forth shuffling of the child. If not handled thoughtfully, this can create instability and confusion for the child. It takes truly dedicated parents to make this kind of co-parenting situation work.

Each parent must also be mindful of how the shared parenting tasks can impinge on other aspects of life, particularly employment commitments. When both parents have participated in parenting fairly equally prior to a separation, the family may have already resolved this issue in a satisfactory way. Attempting to change a long-established allocation of responsibilities, however, may not be simple. Taking the time to map out a realistic calendar together can make this arrangement less stressful to achieve over time.

" If you and your child's other parent are having difficulty agreeing on a plan, consult with an attorney to get a better idea of what a judge might decide. "

Bari Z. Weinberger, Esq.

Custody Type FAQ

Should you fight for primary custody or for more parenting time?

This, of course, is the million-dollar question that rarely has a clear yes or no answer. Depending on how you divided parenting responsibilities prior to separation, it may or may not be clear that one of you has acted as a primary parent over an extensive period of time. If it is clear, primary residential custody may be more or less a forgone conclusion, as the court will most likely award it to the primary parent.

Working out a satisfactory visitation schedule, however, can still be challenging. You may well have a valid claim for more parenting time than the other parent is willing to concede. The way that you present this claim can be instrumental in keeping you out of court: Highlight the best interests of your children and try to present a plan that meets the needs of the children and the other parent, as well as your own needs.

Rather than shouting loudly about your "rights as a parent," emphasize your true desire to be helpful. If possible, propose taking on a greater share of some of the less pleasant responsibilities of parenting in exchange for more time participating in the enjoyable aspects. If there is a concern about younger children spending the night away from their primary home, consider a "phase-in" plan that increases time gradually so that everyone can work up to the adjustment.

If both of you have a history of substantial participation in childcare, and both of you want primary custody, the situation is more complicated. If you feel that you can both continue to work well together for the sake of your children, you may want to try to work out a shared parenting arrangement. In many cases, however, it will be easier for the children to have one primary home while spending substantial time at the home of the other parent. Regardless of which way you decide to go, remember that it will be far easier and far less expensive to resolve the situation between yourselves (with the assistance of a mediator if necessary) than it will be to engage in a costly and unpleasant court battle.

In any high conflict custody or parenting time situation, before letting your emotions get the better of you, be sure to stop and ask yourself some hard questions:

- Is an additional day or half day of parenting per week more about what your children need or more about your own needs?

- Are there ways you can stay involved when you are not technically on "parenting duty," such as attending children's events or having a regular video chat with a child in the evening?

- Would the money you are tempted to invest in a court battle be better invested in something like a college savings account?

> **Practical Tip: Carefully document your custody or parenting-time case.**
> Whether you are seeking primary custody or just a high percentage of parenting time, it is important to document exactly what is currently happening with respect to your children. Keep a detailed log of how much time each parent spends with the children and what responsibilities each parent has.

If you want more responsibility and the other parent is not allowing it, point this out. Be specific about your availability and the types of things you believe you would be able to do for the children. If responsibilities have recently changed, and you believe that past patterns are more indicative of the long-term division of duties, it is also important to point this out and create a retroactive calendar demonstrating the previous state of affairs. This is particularly important if you believe that the other parent is putting on a temporary show of great involvement for the court. A longstanding pattern of non-involvement may cause the court to question whether the new level is likely to be sustainable over time.

In addition to documenting the overall time you spend with children, you will also want to document time spent on specific activities—or time that you would like to spend on specific activities, if you believe that you are being blocked from participation. You can present contributions either in hours per week or percentages of time per parent. The applicable activities will vary depending on a child's age. The following are some examples of specific activities a court may consider in determining custody and visitation issues:

- Feeding
- Shopping for groceries and preparing meals
- Helping with bathing, teeth brushing, or other hygiene related tasks
- Doing laundry
- Shopping for clothing
- Cleaning house
- Assigning and assisting with chores
- Helping with pet care

- Playing games or doing crafts
- Taking vacation trips
- Planning vacations
- Planning parties
- Choosing birthday or holiday gifts
- Helping to buy gifts for child's friends
- Making regular time for conversation
- Teaching a child reading, cooking, or other skills
- Setting limits and enforcing household rules
- Helping with homework
- Participating in bedtime rituals, such as story-reading
- Driving to various appointments and activities
- Accompanying a child on appointments such as doctor and dentist visits
- Attending the child's sporting events, recitals, parent-teacher conferences or other important events
- Taking off work to stay home with a sick child.

If applicable, in addition to specifying all the ways that you have participated as a parent, you may want to point out the percentage of time the other parent has been out of town or otherwise unavailable due to work or other commitments.

Keeping an Open Mind

Custody decisions can pose a multitude of dilemmas that can be very challenging to resolve as they often involve issues of career trajectory and lifestyle, as well as issues of emotional satisfaction. Where patterns have already been in place for some years, practical options may be limited and parents can wind up feeling angry and resentful. One parent may feel trapped between a desire to continue on a stable career path and a desire to take on a greater role as a parent. The other parent may feel trapped between a desire to continue in a role as primary caretaker and a realization that economic realities require an increasing commitment to work outside the home. As both parents come to realize how much more expensive it is to maintain two homes as opposed to one, tensions may escalate still further.

An open mind and willingness to compromise can keep tensions from becoming overwhelming. While cultivating an attitude of compassion and understanding for the other parent's position during this trying period is not always easy, it can be very helpful. Not only will it tend to facilitate a more rapid resolution, but it will also ease the stress that anger and resentment tend to breed.

Negative Effects of High Conflict

A key reason for keeping an open mind and cultivating compassion for your former partner is that this will, ultimately, further your children's best interests. One thing that experts universally agree on is that an environment filled with conflict will negatively impact children. How parents allocate time is less important than that they both strive to maintain a calm and supportive environment. One of the best things that you can do for your children during this stressful period in their lives is to refrain from arguing with your former partner whenever there is any chance that a child could overhear you. Denigrating or "putting down" the other parent in the children's presence is also very damaging. Children will feel safest when they know that their parents are still capable of communicating with one another in a civil manner. They need to be able to love both parents freely and to know that they can rely on both parents for support.

If civility is impossible—and for some former couples it is, at least in the short term—the next best approach is to have as little contact with each other as possible and seek the assistance of a therapist or parenting coach to help you with difficult aspects such as transferring children between homes. For example, parents sometimes arrange for transfers to take place in a neutral location or through an intermediary such as a relative or a babysitter.

Parents who are flexible and are able to communicate with one another have the best chance of being able to manage joint legal custody as well as a physical custody plan that requires a child to frequently change homes. Parents who cannot get along with one another and cannot seem to agree on anything will generally have more success in keeping a calm environment for children with a plan that clearly delineates responsibility for major decisions and requires the child to move less frequently back and forth. Shared legal and physical custody is not usually the best option in this type of situation.

Positive Effects of Consistency

Experts also agree that consistency is important. Children experiencing parental separation or divorce face many changes. Parents can minimize the magnitude of these changes by adhering to the same general division of parenting roles that existed prior to the separation and making any desired changes in a gradual and structured fashion. If parents have shared parenting tasks in a certain way for a considerable amount of time, duplicating the arrangement as closely as possible will generally provide children with the greatest degree of stability.

In some cases, a parent who operated as the more peripheral parent prior to separation takes on a more involved role after separation. A parent who has been the primary caretaker may return to school or take on a full-time job for the first time. These changes can be positive for both parents and children, but they are also likely to be disruptive during the adjustment period. Parents may find it challenging to insist that children adhere to a new parenting schedule if the children are reacting negatively. Enforcing the new schedule can be easier with younger children who are more portable, but younger children may also become more visibly upset. Changes of this nature require patience, commitment, and very close attention to children's individual needs. Parents should also keep in mind that the needs of children change according to age. While stability is important, plans usually need to be modified and adapted as children grow.

Developmental Concerns

At one time, child development experts believed that children under the age of about seven had a much greater need than older children to have their mother fill the function of "primary caretaker." Having another person, even the other parent, interfere with a young child's ability to spend the majority of time with the mother was considered to be damaging to this primary attachment.

This belief led to the dominance of a legal stance often referred to as the "tender years doctrine," which made it almost impossible for a father to obtain primary or equal custody of children six years old or younger. In more recent times, courts have recognized that the tender years doctrine never had much factual support and was resulting in unjustified prejudice against fathers, as well as possibly encouraging parents to view a father's role as unimportant and peripheral. The prevailing modern view is that children of any age are able to form strong bonds with multiple caregivers; that children do best when both parents are actively involved in their lives; and that fathers are quite capable of providing care to very young children. This is a more gender-neutral approach.

The tender years doctrine has been abolished in New Jersey as well as in other states. Under the current law, neither parent begins with an automatic advantage solely on the basis of gender. Parents with concerns may wish to consult with a child development expert, such as a psychologist or a family therapist experienced in working with restructuring families.

FAQ: What is "parental alienation syndrome"?
Parental alienation syndrome (PAS) refers to the existence in a child of strong feelings against one parent resulting from a campaign of alienation (either intentional or accidental) carried out by the other parent. This is a recently identified phenomenon recognized by some courts as an important consideration in child custody decisions.

Mental health experts have recognized three levels of parental alienators:

- **Naïve alienators**—parents who recognize the value to a child of a healthy relationship with each parent but still occasionally denigrate the other parent in the child's presence;

- **Active alienators**—parents who regularly make denigrating remarks about the other parent in a child's presence; and

- **Obsessed alienators**—parents who are intentionally attempting to destroy a child's relationship with the other parent.

While family law judges recognize the potential for damage that exists when one parent expresses hostile feelings toward the other parent in the presence of children, not all judges recognize PAS as a valid syndrome, and those who do tend to focus on the more severe instances of behavior. It can be extremely difficult to determine whether a child's negative feelings toward one parent are due primarily to PAS or are primarily the result of the child's direct interactions with the non-favored parent. Generally speaking, if a child shows unmitigated hostility or resentment towards one parent and there is no objective basis for such feelings, there may be cause for suspicion. If you believe that PAS is a significant factor in your custody case, discuss this with your attorney. You may need to hire a child evaluator to make your case.

Practical Tip: Think twice before attacking your former spouse in court.

Family law courts are very aware that it is possible, and perhaps even common, for a person to be a poor marital partner but a good parent. If you are going through a divorce that includes a custody battle, it may be a great temptation to bring up every way that your spouse behaved improperly during your marriage. The court will not necessarily care if your spouse cheated, lied, or just generally behaved badly, unless such behavior negatively impacted the children or rose to the level of domestic violence. The court also will not care if your spouse has a new love interest, unless there is something about that person that clearly puts the children at risk (or, in the context of dividing finances, if you can prove that your spouse spent marital funds on the relationship). A general character attack without any relevant factual support tends only to make the person launching the attack look bitter and vindictive. Focus your criticisms on your spouse's parenting abilities only. If your spouse did not take on an equal share of parenting responsibilities, point this out. If your spouse did something that put the children at risk, by all means, point that out as well.

Chapter 4

Jurisdiction over Children and Conflicting Custody Orders Between States

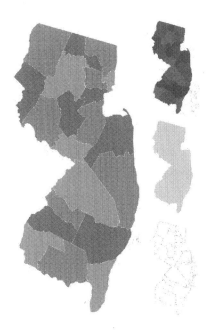

Before a court makes any order for child custody or visitation, a judge will have to decide whether or not the state has jurisdiction (legal authority to hear the case). One parent may object to jurisdiction in a particular state.

In some cases, there is no custody order at all and each parent wants a different state to have jurisdiction. In other cases, one state may have entered custody orders already, and a parent living in a different state is objecting to the validity of the orders.

Many different situations could result in a resident of one state having children subject to custody orders in another state. Often parents have never been married to each other or have been separated for some time. Sometimes one parent has recently left the state with the children and has obtained a custody order in the new state.

There are a myriad of reasons why each parent may want a particular state to have jurisdiction over the case. Some reasons are practical. For example, the closer a parent lives to the court the easier it will be to participate in any court procedures. Other reasons may be based on differences in laws between states regarding issues of child custody and child support. The laws of a particular state may be more favorable for one parent or the other.

Whatever the circumstances, there is a series of factors that a court will consider in deciding whether or not the state has jurisdiction to enter a custody order or whether the court should enforce another state's custody order. These factors are based on the following state and federal laws:

Uniform Child Custody Jurisdiction Act. The Uniform Child Custody Jurisdiction Act (UCCJA) was the original model law that provided states with uniform standards governing custody cases. The law helped ensure that only courts in states with close connections to a child would have the right to make custody decisions. All states and the District of Columbia adopted some form of the UCCJA. Unfortunately, jurisdictional conflicts still occurred because different states enacted slightly different versions of the UCCJA and interpreted its provisions differently. The UCCJA did not prevent more than one state from being able to assume jurisdiction in a child custody case.

Parental Kidnapping Prevention Act and Uniform Child Custody Jurisdiction and Enforcement Act. In 1980, congress enacted a federal law called the Parental Kidnapping Protection Act (PKPA) (Title 28, section 1738A, of the United States Code, explained by Cornell University's Legal Information Institute located at: http://bit.ly/kidnap-act, preempted state laws and ensured that only one state at a time would be able to assume jurisdiction of a custody matter. Among other things, the PKPA provides that once a state properly assumes jurisdiction and enters child custody orders in a case, other states must give those orders full faith and credit.

Original Jurisdiction. The state having original jurisdiction will ordinarily keep jurisdiction unless the child and both parents have since moved to other states. The PKPA also provides that if one state modifies a child custody or visitation order without complying with the terms of the PKPA, another state does not have to give the decision full faith and credit. States have since brought their laws into conformity with the PKPA, primarily by passing a revised version of the UCCJA known as the Uniform Child Custody Jurisdiction and Enforcement Act (UCCJEA). New Jersey's version of the UCCJEA, adopted in 2004, appears at N.J.S.A. 2A:34-53 et seq.

" Before a court makes
any order for child
custody or visitation, a
judge will have to
decide whether or not
the state has jurisdiction. "

Bari Z. Weinberger, Esq.

Analyzing Jurisdiction under the UCCJEA.

Determining whether a state has proper jurisdiction under the UCCJEA can be complicated. It may be critical to consult a family law attorney in a jurisdictional dispute. In general, jurisdiction must be based on one of the following circumstances:

- **Home State**. The most important consideration will be whether or not a state qualifies as the child's "home state." A state is designated as the home state if a child has resided there continuously for the six months preceding the custody action, or if the child resided there for six months prior to leaving the state and one of the parents—or a person acting as a parent—continues to live there. Once a child has lived in a new state for six consecutive months that state ordinarily becomes the new home state.

- **Significant Connections.** Sometimes a child has moved around so much that the home state is difficult to determine. In that case, a court will look at whether or not a child or the child's family has "significant connections" in the state and where most of the evidence relating to the custody claim is located. This could involve questions such as where each parent is employed, where the child has spent the most time, where a child is currently enrolled in school, where a child's pediatrician is located, or where members of the child's extended family live. In some cases, a child will have fairly equal and significant connections with more than one state, but neither state will qualify as the home state. In that case, the question will be which state creates a more convenient forum for the case. Where two courts are both convenient and both willing to accept jurisdiction, one court will have to decline in favor of the other.

- **Emergency.** An emergency situation may exist if a child is currently in one state and has been abandoned or needs protection from abuse or risk of mistreatment. This situation might arise if one parent has left the home state with the child due to fears about domestic violence. Emergency jurisdiction is often accepted by a court on a temporary basis with the understanding that it may be transferred to the home state if the evidence eventually shows that transfer is warranted.

- **Default**. If there is no home state and there does not appear to be another state with significant connections, the state in which the child is currently residing may assume jurisdiction by default.

International Custody Disputes

When one parent is moving from the United States to a completely different country, many of the issues involved in a custody determination are compounded by the greater distance involved and the increased difficulty in getting foreign countries to recognize each other's laws. One of the most traumatic experiences a parent can have is discovering that their child's other parent is planning to move out of the country with the child, or worse, has taken the child to a foreign country with no intention of returning to the United States. The emotional and financial effects of a custody dispute can be multiplied many times over by the impact of an unfamiliar language, unfamiliar culture, and foreign legal system.

The UCCJEA generally provides that states will treat custody orders entered in other countries the same as those entered in the United States, provided that the country had proper jurisdiction to begin with and the custody order does not violate any fundamental human rights. New Jersey's version of the UCCJEA also provides that the foreign court must have given all parties notice and an opportunity to be heard before making the custody determination, and that the custody decision must be based on an evaluation of the best interests of the child.

If one parent has left the country with a child without the consent of the other parent, the parent remaining in the United States can request the home state to enter custody and visitation orders. The major difficulty will generally be with enforcing those orders in a foreign country.

The Hague Convention on the Civil Aspects of International Child Abduction

The Hague Conference on Private International Law is a world organization dedicated to cross-border cooperation. The official Hague Conference website is located at: http://bit.ly/hague-conference. A convention held at The Hague in 1980 addressed the wrongful removal of children from their home country and proposed resolutions addressing such cases. The United States ratified these resolutions in 1988. The U.S. has treaty relationships pursuant to the 1980 convention with more than 65 different countries; however, levels of compliance with the treaties vary from country to country. You can find out more information from the following websites:

- The Hague's Child Abduction Section, located at the official HCCH site: http://bit.ly/hcch-child-abduction.

- The National Center for Missing & Exploited Children, located at the Missing Kids official website: http://bit.ly/center-missing.

- The Office of Children's Issues at the Bureau of Consular Affairs, located at the official US Department of State website: http://bit.ly/child-issues, handles cases regarding children who are wrongfully removed either to or from the United States.

If you are a parent facing an international custody dispute, you will need to consult with a family law attorney who has experience with this type of dispute. If you file an application with The Hague and the result is that a custody hearing is scheduled in a foreign country, you may also need to hire an attorney who can represent you in that country.

Requirements of The Hague Application:
You can file a Hague Application within one year following the wrongful removal of a child who was under the age of 16 at the time of removal from the home country—also called "the country of habitual residence." Information about filing a Hague Application is located at the official Department of State website: http://bit.ly/hagueapplication. The applying parent does not have to have a custody order in effect but must have been exercising a right of custody (actually visiting with and caring for the child to some degree) at the time the child

was removed or retained in the foreign country and must not have consented to the removal or retention.

A parent who has left the country with a child will often return voluntarily when the other parent files a Hague Application. A parent opposing a child's return has the burden of proving that one of the following exceptions applies:

- There is a grave risk that the child's return would expose the child to physical or psychological harm or otherwise place the child in an intolerable situation,

- The child objects to being returned and is sufficiently mature for the court to take this into account, or

- The return would violate fundamental principles of human rights and freedoms according to the country where the child is being held.

Parents should be aware that different courts in different countries will interpret these exceptions in different ways. It is not always possible to predict a result. Mediation can sometimes be an expeditious and effective tool in international cases. You can speak to a State Department case officer at the Office of Children's Issues (toll free at 1 (888) 407-4747) to obtain more information.

Chapter 5

Special Issues in Child Custody for Military Families

Children who have one or more parent serving in the military can be affected by parental separation or divorce in ways that seldom affect children in other types of families. For this reason, many states, including New Jersey, have passed laws addressing the unique circumstances that tend to impact such families.

The following is some brief information about some of these issues and the applicable laws. For more information specific to military families, including two PowerPoint presentations providing an introduction to military divorce in New Jersey and an overview of rights and responsibilities of military parents in New Jersey, see "Military Divorce: New Jersey Divorce When You or Your Spouse is in the Military", located on the official Weinberger Divorce & Family Law Group website at: http://bit.ly/military-guide.

Jurisdiction

Jurisdiction over children is especially likely to be a concern in a child custody dispute where one or both parents are serving in the military. This can be particularly challenging if a child has been residing overseas for more than six months with a military parent. Even if the child is a United States citizen, jurisdiction may belong to the foreign country, and the parents will have to either enter into a parenting agreement or apply to the foreign court for a custody order. This is a complicated matter requiring the assistance of an experienced attorney. Establishing jurisdiction will be of greatest concern during the initial order stage, as the court with original jurisdiction over children will retain jurisdiction for purposes of later modifications in most cases. New Jersey law specifically provides that even if a child will be living out of the state under a temporary modification order, New Jersey will retain home state jurisdiction over the child.

" Jurisdiction over children is especially likely to be a concern in a child custody dispute where one or both parents are serving in the military. "

Bari Z. Weinberger, Esq.

Parenting Plans and Deployment

Many states, including New Jersey, have passed laws addressing the special need for flexibility in child custody arrangements and parenting plans when one or both parents are in the service. Deployments can be unpredictable, sometimes involve short notice, and often require all members of a family to make difficult adjustments. Military parents have had to face special concerns regarding loss of custody or parenting time during deployment, especially deployment overseas. A New Jersey law which became effective in 2013 (N.J.S.A. § 9:2-12.1) essentially prevents courts from making permanent child custody decisions while a parent is on active military duty. Courts must wait until at least 90 days after a deployment ends before entering permanent child custody orders in a case or making permanent changes to any custody and parenting time orders already in existence. In addition, a non-deploying parent cannot base a request for a change in custody or parenting time solely on a deploying parent's absence due to military service.

If one parent is deployed overseas, this does not automatically mean that children will have to stay in the United States with the other parent. In some cases, the decision that will be in the best interests of a child whose parent is about to be deployed overseas will be a temporary arrangement that allows the child to accompany the parent. This will depend on an analysis of all relevant circumstances, including whether or not the deploying parent has been the primary caretaker, what kind of arrangements the child's other parent or an alternate caretaker could provide, and the conditions the child would encounter in the country of deployment. While safety is certainly a concern in some locations, most military bases overseas have their own daycare facilities, and there may be unique opportunities for enrichment when children are permitted to accompany a parent overseas.

In situations where children will not accompany the deploying parent, New Jersey's new law protects the relationships between children and deploying parents by providing that any temporary modifications to parenting plans during deployment must allow a deploying parent to exercise custody or parenting time during periods of leave and must expire automatically when the deploying parent returns. At that point the original orders will go back into effect unless the non-deploying parent can demonstrate that this is against the child's best interests.

Another important feature of the New Jersey law is that it allows a deploying parent, in an appropriate case, to delegate parenting time during deployment to any person who has a close personal relationship with both the parent and the child. This is often in the child's best interests. For example, if a child ordinarily lives with the deploying parent and a step-parent or a grandparent, the step-parent or grandparent may be able to continue providing care for the child in the same home during the deployment, preventing the necessity of the child moving to the home of the non-custodial parent, which, depending on the circumstances, might prove more disruptive for the child.

Expedited or Electronic Hearings

New Jersey's current law also allows parents who are facing an imminent deployment that would prevent them from appearing personally or fully participating in an initial child custody or parenting time hearing or evaluation to request an expedited hearing date before the deployment without waiving their right under the SCRA to request a delay or stay of proceedings during the deployment.

Servicemembers involved in New Jersey child custody and parenting matters are expressly allowed to present testimony and evidence by electronic means such as telephone or Internet conference.

Chapter 6

Grandparents and Other Third Party Custody and Visitation

Laws allowing third parties (i.e. grandparents, same-sex partners, step-parents, or anyone else who is neither a biological parent nor an adoptive parent), to obtain rights of custody or visitation vary from state to state.

However, the United States Supreme Court decision in the case of Troxel v. Granville (2000), located via Google Scholar at: http://bit.ly/troxel-granville, has affected the way that states have interpreted and revised their own laws in recent years. In that case, the Supreme Court held that natural parents have a constitutionally protected right to decide how to raise their children, and that third parties (in this case a child's grandparents) seeking visitation with a child over a parent's objections must demonstrate that the child would be harmed by a denial of visitation. The Court determined that the federal constitution prevents states from interfering with parents' rights unless such interference is necessary to prevent harm or potential harm to a child.

Although the *Troxel* case specifically concerned grandparent visitation, the idea that parents have a fundamental constitutional right to decide how to raise their children must be taken into account in any situation dealing with third party custody or visitation. This is an evolving area of the law. If you are attempting to gain custody or visitation over the objections of one or both of a child's parents, or if you are a parent opposing someone else's claim for custody or visitation, you should consult with an attorney to clarify your status given the current state of the law and the exact circumstances of your case.

By far the best way to resolve such situations is through an agreement between the legal parents and the third party. Only in rare cases does a parent actually wish to block contact entirely, and with cooperation and understanding, the parties can often reach a solution that serves the child's best interests and that everyone who cares for the child finds acceptable. In some situations, however, agreement will not be possible. For those who find themselves unable to reach an acceptable agreement, the following general outline of the current state of the law may be helpful:

Third Party Custody:

New Jersey law provides that anyone interested in a child's welfare can file a custody case. The majority of third party custody cases involve grandparents, same-sex partners, or step-parents. In the typical scenario, the third party has been acting as a parent to a child either in conjunction with one of the child's legal parents or in place of the child's legal parents. A change of circumstances, such as a relationship break-up, or an improvement in a parent's ability to care for a child, causes the parent to attempt to limit or end the relationship between the child and the third party, and the third party files a custody case in family court.

Whenever a legal (biological or adoptive) parent contests an award of custody to a third party, the law starts with a presumption in favor of the legal parent based on the parent's constitutional rights. For a third party to overcome this presumption, there must be compelling circumstances. New Jersey courts have found compelling circumstances in two basic types of situations:

- the parent is unfit, has committed gross misconduct, or has abandoned the child, or some other exceptional circumstance exists that creates a risk of physical or psychological harm to the child, or

- the third party has become the "psychological parent" of the child.

" **New Jersey provides that anyone interested in a child's welfare can file a custody case.** "

Bari Z. Weinberger, Esq.

Parental unfitness or abandonment:

Cases concerning unfitness or abandonment often involve temporary arrangements made for a child's safety. A social services agency will generally be involved and the consent of the parents will not be required due to the immediate risk of physical or psychological harm to the child. However, a temporary custody arrangement will ordinarily become permanent only if the parent's rights are terminated through a court process. In New Jersey, the agency charged with protection of children in such cases is the New Jersey Division of Child Protection and Permanency (DCP&P), located at the official Department of Children and Families website: http://bit.ly/nj-dcpp. The DCP&P is a division of the New Jersey Department of Children and Families. This is the same agency formerly known as the New Jersey Division of Youth and Family Services (DYFS); the name was changed in early 2012 to better reflect its mission. You can find additional information about DCP&P and termination of parental rights later in this chapter.

Sometimes a parent who is experiencing difficulties feels incapable of caring for a child and voluntarily turns the care of the child over to a third party. If the third party cares for the child in the parent's place for an extended period of time, the case may develop into a psychological parenting case.

Psychological Parents:

In a psychological parenting case, the legal parent does not need to be unfit because the third party's custody claim is based on the legal parent's consent to and encouragement of the third party's parenting role. While most third party cases are brought by same-sex partners, step-parents, grandparents, or other close relatives, any third party who satisfies the requirements can be declared a psychological parent. It is not enough for the third party to show that the best interests of a child favor granting custody or visitation to a psychological parent over the objections of the legal parent. The party attempting to establish a psychological parenting claim must specifically prove each of the following four elements:

- the biological or adoptive parent consented to, and fostered, the third party's formation of a parent-like relationship with the child,

- the third party and the child lived together in the same household,

- the third party assumed significant responsibility for the child's care, education and development, including contributing toward the child's support (financial or otherwise) without any expectation of compensation, and

- the third party functioned in a parental role for long enough to establish a bonded, dependent, parent-child type of relationship.

Rights of the Psychological Parent:

New Jersey courts consider third parties who have demonstrated all the required elements of a psychological parent claim to stand "in parity"—that is, on equal ground—with a biological or adoptive parent in a custody case. This means that a court will determine custody disputes between legal and psychological parents by analyzing the best interests of the child according to all the factors that would apply to a custody dispute between two legal parents.

There are some limitations on the rights and responsibilities of psychological parents, however. The psychological parent who has been granted custody will not necessarily have the same rights as a legal parent with regard to autonomy over all decisions regarding the child. The rationale for this premise is that the rights of the psychological parent in relation to those of a legal parent depend on the legal parent having voluntarily turned authority over to the psychological parent. This affects the rights between the legal parent and the psychological parent, but it does not confer the constitutional rights of a natural parent on a psychological parent, and therefore does not give the psychological parent any elevated status in disputes with other third parties. So, for example, if another third party (e.g., the other set of grandparents) is requesting visitation with a child over the objection of a psychological parent, the court will analyze the situation according to the best interests of the child and will not begin with any presumption in favor of the psychological parent. The additional third party does not have to prove that denying visitation would result in harm to the child.

Another distinction between legal and psychological parents is that the latter are not subject to the New Jersey Child Support Guidelines. If, however, a psychological parent has voluntarily provided a child with financial support, a court might order the continuation of such support.

Death of Custodial Parent

If a child's custodial parent dies, the surviving parent has a rebuttable presumption of custody, but custody does not automatically revert to the non-custodial parent. The parent must obtain a family court order transferring custody. A third party objecting to the transfer would have to demonstrate that the surviving parent is unfit, has committed gross misconduct, or has abandoned the child, or that some other exceptional circumstance exists. If one of the latter conditions is present, a court will use a best interest analysis.

Grandparent and Sibling Visitation

New Jersey has a statute that specifically addresses visitation rights of grandparents and siblings. The statute states that a grandparent or sibling residing in New Jersey can apply for a visitation order and must prove that the visitation is in the best interests of the child, based on the following factors:

- the relationship between the child and the applicant,

- the relationship between each of the child's parents, or the person the child is living with, and the applicant,

- the amount of time which has passed since the child last had contact with the applicant,

- the effect that the visitation would have on the relationship between the child and the child's parents or the person the child is living with,

- if the parents are divorced or separated, the parenting time arrangement between the parents,

- the good faith of the applicant in filing the application,

- any history of physical, emotional or sexual abuse or neglect by the applicant, and

- any other factor relevant to the child's best interests.

The statute also states that if an applicant has been a full-time caretaker of a child in the past, this will be sufficient evidence that visitation would be in a child's best interests, unless there is also evidence to the contrary.

The wording of statute N.J.S.A. 9:2-7.1 appears to give grandparents and siblings a special right to seek visitation. Indeed, prior to the United States Supreme Court decision in *Troxel v. Granville* (2000), discussed above, New Jersey courts did interpret this statute to require that grandparents or siblings applying for visitation rights need show only that the visitation would be in a child's best interests. If the visitation was in the child's best interests, a court could disregard even a fit parent's decision not to allow it. Since *Troxel v. Granville*, however, New Jersey courts have required even grandparent and sibling applicants to show first that visitation is necessary to avoid harm to the child.

Issues under the New Jersey statute most frequently involve grandparents. Sibling cases may come up in adoption or foster care situations, but a child's legal guardian will rarely have a significant reason to want to prevent siblings from visiting with one another. There is much more likely to be a power struggle involved in a dispute between a parent and a grandparent (and particularly between a parent and a grandparent-in-law).

If a court decides that a grandparent has demonstrated that visitation is necessary to avoid harm to the grandchild, then the parent must propose a schedule. If the grandparent does not accept the structure of the schedule, the court will decide whether the schedule meets the child's best interests according to the factors listed in the visitation statute. A claim that the schedule provides the child with insufficient time with the grandparent would still require proof that the inadequacy would be likely to cause harm to the child. If the court agrees, then the court will develop a new visitation schedule that is adequate to meet the child's best interests based on the statutory factors (*Moriarty v. Bradt*, 177 N.J. 84 2003, located via Google Scholar at: http://bit.ly/moriarty-bradt).

If the above analysis seems convoluted and confusing, it is because it represents an effort to accommodate two competing interests that are both important. The courts and the legislature recognize that in most cases grandparents and siblings have special relationships with children that are worthy of protection. The United States Supreme Court, however, has afforded constitutional protection only to legal parents.

For a grandparent to prevail over the wishes of a legal parent in this type of scenario, the grandparent must show that there is such a close relationship between the child and the grandparent that the child would suffer if the relationship were not allowed to continue. This will not be easy to prove. The grandparent must indicate specific ways that the child would suffer. Vague statements that the child will lose loving interactions or happy memories will not generally be enough. The first step will be to establish the significance and closeness of the current relationship between the grandparent and the child. An expert opinion may be necessary to show that the loss of the relationship would be emotionally damaging to the child.

Chapter 7

Loss of Rights to Custody or Visitation

A parent's actions can affect custody and visitation rights on many levels. Evaluating the best interests of a child often requires a court to scrutinize parenting skills and parent-child relationships very closely. In the vast majority of cases, however, the court will permit both parents to have frequent contact with their children.

Only in very unusual circumstances will a court drastically limit contact. These situations generally involve concern for a child's safety, or sometimes, concern for the safety of the child's other parent.

In some cases, a court will impose only a temporary safeguard, such as requiring a third party to supervise visitation until the parent has satisfied certain requirements—completing a drug rehabilitation program, for example. In the most extreme situations, a parent may lose all rights to custody and visitation.

A denial of custody and visitation is not the same thing as a termination of parental rights. Even when a court awards one parent sole legal and physical custody, the other parent is still obligated to pay child support. The parent also retains the right to return to court at a later time and request a modification of the custody and visitation order. Terminating the parental rights of one parent is rarely necessary when parents are separated or divorced, provided that the other parent is capable of providing full–time, permanent care for the child. Termination of parental rights requires a separate court process with very specific requirements. You can find more information on this process later in this book.

Situations involving limitations on custody or visitation include:

Criminal Convictions:

A New Jersey court cannot award custody or visitation to any person, including a parent, who has been convicted of specific criminal acts, unless the court first finds clear and convincing evidence that it would be in the best interests of the child to award custody or visitation to the convicted person. The criminal acts include:

- sexual assault,
- criminal sexual contact, and
- endangering a child's welfare.

Criminal acts that endanger a child's welfare include child abuse or neglect, as well as crimes involving sexual conduct that is likely to be morally harmful to children. New Jersey law defines child abuse or neglect to include any of the following:

- causing serious physical or emotional harm to a child, or allowing another person to cause such harm,

- creating a risk of physical harm to a child, or allowing another person to create such risk,

- sexually abusing a child, or allowing another person to sexually abuse a child,

- harming a child, or creating a risk of harm to a child, by failing to provide proper care,

- using excessive physical punishment on a child, or

- abandoning a child.

A judge who decides that a caretaker has failed to protect a child from a serious risk of harm can find that the caretaker abused or neglected the child even if the child has not actually suffered harm. Because of this broad definition, competent attorney representation is critical in a child abuse or neglect case.

" A parent's actions can affect custody and visitation rights on so many levels. "

Bari Z. Weinberger, Esq.

Action by the New Jersey Division of Child Protection and Permanency (DCP&P):

In situations that do not involve a pre-existing criminal conviction, a limitation on custody or visitation is likely to involve action by the New Jersey Division of Child Protection and Permanency (DCP&P) located at the official DCP&P website: http://bit.ly/nj-dcpp. Laws protecting children require a wide variety of individuals to report suspected child abuse or neglect to a social service agency. In some states the reporting laws apply only to certain professionals. In New Jersey, the laws are written broadly to require any person with reasonable cause to believe that a child has been abused or neglected to report the abuse or neglect to DCP&P. Under New Jersey law, a person who fails to report known child abuse or neglect can be fined up to $1,000 and can be imprisoned for up to six months.

Reporting Child Abuse or Neglect:

DCP&P maintains a reporting hotline (1-877 NJ ABUSE) or (1-877-652-2873), and callers may anonymously report information. Anyone who reports abuse or neglect "in good faith" is immune from civil or criminal penalties as a result of making the report. Hotline responders will ask a caller to identify the child and the alleged abuser and provide details of the behavior causing the concern, including the place and time the behavior occurred, how the caller learned about the behavior, any known current or previous injury to the child, the child's and the alleged abuser's current locations, and any ongoing or immediate risk to the child.

Accusations Made by a Parent against the Child's Other Parent:

In cases of contested custody and visitation, the child abuse reporting laws protect a parent who mistakenly reports that the other parent is abusing or neglecting a child, provided that the suspicions of abuse or neglect are reasonable. A parent who knowingly makes a false allegation against the other parent is not only harming the other parent but is acting against the best interests of the child. This can indeed have serious adverse repercussions for the parent making a false report.

Unfortunately, both child abuse and neglect and false reporting of abuse and neglect sometimes occur in contested custody cases. If you are a parent in a contested custody case and you believe that the other parent has falsely accused you of child abuse or neglect, you should seek attorney assistance as soon as possible.

DCP&P Investigation:

DCP&P investigates all reports of child abuse or neglect by any person having custodial care of a child (including not only parents, but also teachers, babysitters, and other caretakers). The investigation will begin immediately if serious or ongoing abuse is a concern, or within 24 hours in other cases of alleged abuse. Investigations of neglect claims ordinarily begin within 72 hours of a report.

Depending on the level of investigation a case requires, DCP&P may collect information from various sources. A caseworker will conduct home visits and interviews with the child, the child's household members, and other people who may be involved with the child, such as teachers, physicians, or school counselors. The agency may examine school and medical records, and may conduct medical evaluations or other assessments if necessary.

If an investigator determines that a caregiver has harmed a child or placed a child at substantial risk of harm, DCP&P may open a case in superior court while continuing with its own investigation and administrative findings. The court action will ordinarily include a request to allow DCP&P to supervise the family and provide services. In the most serious cases, DCP&P may request an order removing the children from the home.

DCP&P does not initiate criminal cases, although in some situations, a criminal case may be based on the same circumstances as a civil case. New Jersey law requires DCP&P to report substantiated cases of child abuse and serious neglect to the county prosecutor. In such cases, law enforcement officials will coordinate any criminal investigation with DCP&P.

DCP&P Services:

DCP&P does not aim to punish parents. The goal is to protect children; in most cases this means helping parents to become better caretakers. The agency is authorized to offer struggling parents a wide range of services, including day care, homemaker care, parent education classes, individual and group counseling, and even financial assistance. In most cases, DCP&P will respond to an initial report of abuse or neglect by offering services on a voluntary basis. Only if a parent refuses services or a child appears to be at very high risk will the court become involved. A court order can permit DCP&P to provide mandatory services with home supervision and periodic monitoring, and in the most serious cases, to place children outside the home.

Administrative Substantiation of Abuse or Neglect:

DCP&P makes its own formal administrative findings, independent of any court action, in cases of abuse or neglect. If the agency concludes that a parent or caregiver has abused or neglected a child, the charges are said to be "substantiated." DCP&P must notify the parent or caregiver of any substantiated charges, as this decision can have serious consequences. DCP&P will provide the information to police and place the offender's name in the New Jersey Child Abuse Registry. This can restrict the offender's ability to engage in certain activities, including employment, that involve contact with children, the disabled or the elderly.

A parent or caregiver who disagrees with a DCP&P decision has 20 days to appeal it and request an administrative hearing. A parent or caregiver who is already a defendant in a court case based on the allegations of abuse or neglect should notify the attorney handling the court case of the substantiation decision immediately.

The DCP&P Process in Superior Court

If DCP&P initiates a court procedure against you as a parent suspected of child abuse or neglect, the case will generally proceed through the following steps:

Order to Show Cause and Complaint:

DCP&P will open the case by filing an Order to Show Cause and a Complaint. These papers will explain why DCP&P believes that you abused or neglected your child and may request temporary removal of the child from your home. The court sets a preliminary hearing date when the initial papers are filed. If DCP&P removes your child from the home on an emergency basis, the agency must file a Complaint within 72 business hours, and you will be entitled to have a preliminary hearing at the time of filing.

Preliminary Hearing:

At the preliminary hearing, the judge decides whether DCP&P can continue with the case and whether the child should live outside of the home while the case goes forward. In some cases, a judge will allow a child to stay at home if satisfactory supervision is available, or if the abusive parent leaves the home. The judge may order services such as psychological evaluations, substance abuse testing or treatment, or domestic violence services. The service providers will issue reports and recommendations to the court on a periodic basis.

Discovery:

If the judge decides that the case should go forward, there will be a period during which both sides gather additional information. This is called "discovery". The judge may also schedule a status or case management conference to be held sometime after the preliminary hearing, so that the judge can keep track of where the parties are in the discovery process.

Fact-Finding Hearing:

Discovery is usually followed by a fact-finding hearing, which is equivalent to a trial. At the fact-finding hearing DCP&P will present evidence of the claims against you, and you will have the right to present a defense. Preparing for this hearing with an attorney is the best way to protect your interests.

Dispositional Hearing:

At the conclusion of the fact-finding hearing, the judge will decide whether you have abused or neglected your child and will explain the reasons for the decision. If the judge does find abuse or neglect, there will be another hearing, called a dispositional hearing, during which the judge will order steps you must complete, such as participation in counseling, substance abuse treatment or parenting classes. The judge will also decide whether or not the child may live in the home while these steps are completed. You have 45 days following a dispositional hearing to file an appeal.

Review Hearings:

If the court has ordered services at the dispositional hearing, there will be additional review hearings to monitor progress. The court will dismiss the case and allow the child to live in your home only if it determines that the home is stable and safe. It is very important to comply with everything the court orders at the dispositional hearing.

Permanency Hearing:

If the case stays open for more than a year, the court will conduct a permanency hearing. At this time DCP&P will present a plan for a permanent solution that provides a stable long-term living arrangement for the child. You have the right to present an alternative plan. If DCP&P does not believe that your home can become a safe place for your child, there is a risk that they will file a separate court case to terminate your parental rights. Your attorney can give you more information about this risk, as well as about all potential permanent solutions.

Steps to Take If You are Accused of Child Abuse or Neglect

- Obtain an attorney as soon as possible. Having attorney representation from the very beginning of any DCP&P involvement is the best way to ensure that you will have adequate assistance throughout this difficult process. Your attorney may be able to prevent the matter from turning into a court case. If DCP&P does file a case in court, the agency will ordinarily name both parents, even when only one parent has been accused of abuse or neglect. In most cases each parent needs to have a separate attorney.

- Be aware that a Deputy Attorney General will represent DCP&P, and the court will appoint an attorney for the child, called a Law Guardian, or a "guardian ad litem". If you cannot afford an attorney to defend your court case, you may qualify for representation from the Office of Parental Representation (OPR), a unit of the New Jersey Office of the Public Defender. OPR has several regional offices located throughout the state. Consult the resources at the end of this chapter for additional information about OPR. If you do not have an attorney before your preliminary hearing, you can ask the judge to postpone the hearing to give you time to find one.

- Cooperate in developing a plan to help your child. In most cases, the law requires DCP&P to try to keep your family together and to work with you to develop a plan for this. Take advantage of any services DCP&P

offers your family. If you believe that you need more help, ask for it. Your caseworker and your attorney can help you determine what your family needs. If DCP&P wants to place your child outside the home and you have relatives who can care for your child, let DCP&P know this immediately. In most cases, if DCP&P removes a child from the home, the parents have a right to visit the child. Your attorney can make sure that you get the best visitation plan possible.

Chapter 8

Modifying and Enforcing Parenting Orders

The court entering initial parenting orders will maintain jurisdiction over all matters relating to parenting until the children attain financial independence.

This means that the court retains the power to make changes in child custody or visitation arrangements whenever there is a substantial change in circumstances after entry of the initial orders. In general, courts will not modify orders post-judgment unless the change in circumstances has already occurred and is expected to continue indefinitely or for at least a considerable length of time.

The majority of issues concerning child custody and visitation that arise post-divorce occur when:

- one party fails to carry out the orders of the court, or
- a change of circumstances justifies a modification of the court's orders.

This chapter provides more information about each of these potential situations and can help you get started with a plan in the event that you find yourself facing one of them after your divorce.

Modifying Parenting Orders

Once a custody and visitation or parenting time order is in place, whether implemented by agreement or through court intervention, a parent applying for a modification must prove that circumstances have changed substantially since the date of the original decision. A court will consider all factors relevant to the best interests of the child, just as in an original custody determination.

Courts generally require parents to make their best efforts to work out an acceptable new plan through negotiation or mediation prior to bringing the matter to court. A parent who has minimal visitation time and is simply requesting an increase will usually have a greater chance of success, as this type of change is in conformity with the general policy in favor of a child having frequent and continuing contact with both parents. A request for a change of the primary residential parent or a change from sole to joint custody will require proof that the change is necessary to further the child's best interests.

Relocation Cases

One of the most difficult issues that separating or divorcing parents may face occurs when one parent wishes to move a considerable distance away from the other parent's residence, particularly if the desired move is out of the state, or even more drastically, out of the country.

Relocation and job loss are common occurrences. Finding a new job can be difficult and often requires investigating prospects throughout the country rather than just in the immediate neighborhood. In addition to dealing with such potential economic stressors, divorced parents who have lost the emotional support of marriage frequently wish to regain closer ties with family members who may live in different states. Living near extended family members can often be a great help to a single parent in need of childcare, as well as a source of emotional support. Many parents remarry and wish to relocate so that the new spouse can take advantage of a lucrative job opportunity.

Fortunately, recent technological advances have made it far less difficult for a committed parent to remain in close contact with a child even while living a considerable distance away. Modes of communication such as cell phones, laptop computers and webcams are increasingly affordable and common.

New Jersey law begins with the premise that divorced or separated parents of minor children born in New Jersey cannot move out of state with the child unless the other parent agrees or a court determines that the relocation is permissible.

If the parents agree that one of them needs to relocate, the other parent can sign a consent order allowing the moving parent to remove the child from the state. In a situation where one parent opposes the move and the parents cannot come to an agreement even after negotiation or mediation, an arbitrator or a judge will decide the issue after a full hearing.

The parent who wishes to move with the child must file a motion in Family Court and obtain a court order granting removal. Whether or not the court will allow the child to move with the parent depends on many factors.

Relocation Cases With Custody Orders:

New Jersey law states that a divorced or separated parent who wishes to move out of New Jersey with a child must demonstrate "cause" if the proposed move is against the wishes of the other parent and the child was either born in New Jersey or has lived in New Jersey for at least five years. N.J.S.A. § 9:2-2.

The meaning of "cause" has been the subject of much debate. For many years, the New Jersey Supreme Court hesitated to put too heavy a burden on custodial parents (or parents of primary residence) who wished to relocate with children, reasoning that undue restrictions would effectively prevent such parents from having the same post-divorce opportunities as noncustodial parents. This approach relied on social research that closely linked children's positive post-divorce adjustment with the psychological well-being of their custodial parents.

Between 2001 and 2017, the New Jersey Supreme Court case of *Baures v. Lewis*, 770 A.2d 214 (N.J. 2001) controlled relocation cases in the state, granting a preference to parents with primary residential custody who wished to move out of New Jersey with a child. In *Bisbing v. Bisbing*, 166 A.3d 1155 (N.J. 2017), however, the court reversed itself, replacing the preference with a pure "best interests" analysis.

While *Baures* is no longer the law, a familiarity with that case can help parents understand the evolution and current state of relocation law in New Jersey.

Relocation Law Prior to 2017
Parents with Joint Legal Custody and One Primary Residential Parent:

The *Baures* court believed that the main factor impacting a child's successful adjustment to a new home state was the happiness and success of that child's primary custodial parent. A custodial parent who wished to move did not have to show that the move would necessarily present any real advantage to either parent or child. The parent could present a prima facie case for relocation simply by producing evidence that there was a good faith reason for the move, and that the move would not be harmful to the child.

Demonstrating Good Faith
- A "good faith" reason was essentially *any* genuine reason that was not motivated by a desire to keep the child away from the other parent.

Demonstrating Lack of Harm

- "Lack of harm" meant that educational and recreational opportunities for the child in the new location were at least comparable to those in the original location.
- The custodial parent was also required to produce a new parenting schedule sufficient to nurture and maintain the connection between the child and the noncustodial parent.

Opposing a Move-Away under *Baures*

Once a custodial parent met the initial burden of proof, a noncustodial parent opposing the move had to present evidence that the move was *not* really in good faith, that the new location would *not* be a positive environment for the child, or that the proposed parenting plan would *not* be effective in allowing the child and the noncustodial parent to maintain a close relationship. A court assessing a contested relocation under *Baures* would hold a hearing to consider twelve factors listed by the court, to the extent that such factors were relevant to the issues of good faith and lack of harm to the child.

Parents with Joint Legal Custody Who Also Share Physical Custody

Baures also clarified that one parent could not make a prima facie case for relocation if a court found initially that parents shared both legal and physical custody. Instead, the court would hold a full hearing to consider whether or not an analysis of the best interests of the child factors set forth in N.J.S.A. 9:2-4(c) (the same factors applicable to an initial determination of custody and visitation) would support a change in the current custodial arrangement to designate the moving parent as primary residential custodian. Only if this change was granted would the court then apply the relocation analysis described above.

In determining the existence of shared custody, courts looked at a family's day-to-day interactions as well as legal agreements and court orders. Shared parenting time was critical, but so was each parent's assumption of primary caretaking responsibilities, such as transporting children to and from school and extracurricular activities, assisting with homework assignments, planning and preparing meals, and attending to medical and health needs.

Relocation Law Since 2017

The *Bisbing* court overturned *Baures,* holding that judges must apply the best interests factor in *every* relocation case. In justifying the reversal, the court noted that research subsequent to *Baures* had not clearly supported the beliefs underpinning that decision. There was no solid consensus regarding the impact of a custodial parent's success or failure on a child's positive or negative reaction to relocation. On the contrary, the court concluded, all children are different and might respond in varying ways to a move.

The Best Interests of the Child

Under current law, therefore, the factors that must be analyzed when determining whether or not to permit a parent to relocate with the child are:

- The parents' ability to agree, communicate and cooperate in matters relating to the child;

- The parents' willingness to accept custody and any history of unwillingness to allow visitation that is not based upon substantiated abuse;
- The interactions and relationship of the child with its parents and siblings;
- Any history of domestic violence;
- The safety of the child and the safety of either parent from physical abuse by the other parent;
- The preference of the child if the child is of sufficient age and capacity to reason so as to make an intelligent decision;
- The needs of the child;
- The stability of the home environment offered;
- The quality and continuity of the child's education;
- The fitness of the parents;
- The geographical proximity of the parents' homes;
- The extent and quality of the time spent with child prior to or subsequent to the separation;
- The parents' employment responsibilities; and
- The age and number of children.

N.J.S.A. 9:2-4 (c)

Relocation Cases without Custody Orders:

Unfortunately, it is not that unusual for one parent's plans to move away to come as a complete surprise to the other parent. This can happen even when parents are living together or married. One parent may be under the impression that the other is only taking a temporary trip with the child; only after an extended period of time does it become clear that the trip was intended to be permanent all along. The parent who is planning to relocate sometimes feels justified in assuming custody of the child as the primary caretaker, or may mistakenly believe that the chances of success in a custody conflict will be better if the parent moves first and works out the details later.

If there is no custody order in effect, there is ordinarily nothing to stop a parent who lives with a child from taking the child on a short-term trip away from home; however, parents who do this with the intention of staying away permanently may be interfering with the relationship between the child and the other parent and will usually be doing themselves much more harm than good in an eventual custody determination. Courts consider this type of behavior to be very much against a child's best interests. There are exceptions, such as domestic violence situations, where the behavior may be temporarily justified for the safety and well-being of one parent and the child, but these circumstances are not common.

If you are a parent who legitimately fears that the other parent may harm you or your child, you can visit Weinberger Divorce & Family Law Group's website for free information about domestic violence, located at: http://bit.ly/wlg-domestic-violence. Information available on the website includes detailed instructions on how to file a restraining order, located at: http://bit.ly/restraining-orders.

If either you or your child is in physical danger, do not hesitate to take action. Call the police or go to the police station and take the children with you. You can also contact a Domestic Violence Shelter or a New Jersey domestic violence attorney for immediate assistance.

If you are a parent whose spouse or partner has left home with your child, or is remaining away from home with your child against your wishes, you should take action as soon as possible to protect your child and your relationship

" The court retains the power to make changes in child custody or visitation arrangements whenever there is a substantial change of circumstances. "

Bari Z. Weinberger, Esq.

with the child. If there is no custody order in effect, you can go to court to obtain orders for temporary custody and visitation. If the other parent disregards a court order to return the child, you can consider pursuing parental kidnapping charges. This is an extremely drastic step, however, and it will always escalate conflict. Be sure that you have consulted a family law attorney and pursued all available options before filing charges against the other parent.

General Considerations in Relocation Cases

It is still too soon to know exactly how the new analysis will play out in the courts. Some parents with primary physical custody may continue to have an easier time than other parents in demonstrating that relocation would be in a child's best interests. This will no longer be due to any automatic edge granted to a custodial parent, however. It will result *only* if an application of the factors favors that parent. For example, if a custodial parent spends by far the most time with the child and assumes a much larger share of parenting responsibilities, then "the extent and quality of the time spent with child" would weigh in that parents favor. On the other hand, factors like "quality and continuity of the child's education" might weigh in favor of not permitting the child to move. A court will look at all relevant factors. A parent of primary residence now has the same burden of proof as any other parent.

Regardless of the particular type of custody arrangement, a parent arguing against a move will need to demonstrate a close relationship with the child and argue that the proposed move will drastically alter that relationship to the child's detriment. A parent who has been only peripherally involved in a child's life before the move was announced, or who appears motivated more by self-interest than the interests of a child, will be less likely to succeed in preventing the move.

Parents on both sides of a relocation dispute must be aware that these cases are often time-consuming and expensive. The court may appoint a mental health professional to evaluate the potential effects of a proposed move on the child as well as the adequacy of proposed alternative visitation plans. Sometimes parents who disagree with the evaluator's opinion wish to hire their own custody experts as well.

This can be extremely expensive and will not necessarily improve the parent's chances. If each parent hires an expert, the opinions may end up cancelling each other out and then the judge might appoint a third expert. Occasionally an expert one parent has hired will even wind up lending support to the other side. Before you consider hiring any expert, be sure to thoroughly familiarize yourself with the expert's previous opinions. Experts may have a significant bias in one direction or another. Your attorney can give you additional information regarding the necessity of hiring experts and the type of expert that might be helpful to your case.

Finally, any parent dealing with a relocation situation should be aware that changes in this area of the law have been relatively frequent in recent years. To be certain of the current state of the law, you should always consult a family law attorney.

FAQ: What can I do if the other parent tries to move with the kids without my consent?
Contact an attorney immediately for assistance. You will need to file a motion in Family Court as soon as possible. If the other parent has left the state with the children without providing you with contact information, do not

hesitate to call the police as well. The sooner you get help trying to locate the children, the more likely it is that they will be located without delay.

Motions to Enforce Litigant's Rights

When one party fails to follow the terms of a court order, the other party's primary remedy will be to file a motion to enforce litigant's rights. This type of motion allows a party to ask the court to enforce previous orders and impose penalties on the party failing to comply, including, when appropriate, monetary sanctions. In the family law context, one former spouse may use this type of motion to compel the other to pay child support or alimony, as well as comply with the terms of custody and visitation orders.

Enforcing Custody and Visitation Orders

Parents have a legal duty to comply with court-ordered parenting plans. In most cases, this duty includes encouraging a child to spend time with the other parent. On the one hand, parents need to maintain a certain degree of flexibility to make a parenting plan work; running off to court after every minor violation of the terms of a plan is not conducive to a peaceful co-parenting relationship. On the other hand, consistent or extreme violations may be best addressed through legal channels.

Interference with custody or visitation includes not only total prevention of contact between a child and a parent, but also more subtle behavior such as blocking telephone or email contact, or consistently scheduling a child's appointments and activities during scheduled visitation time. Even talking about the other parent in a negative manner is a form of interference. Children are very impressionable; hearing one parent continually complain about the other can deeply affect the parent-child relationship. A judge who finds that a child is refusing to spend time with one parent due to behavior of the other is likely to impose penalties on the interfering parent, and may consider whether the child's best interests would be served by changing the current parenting arrangement, including potentially changing the designation of who will serve as the primary residential parent.

If you find yourself in a situation where your child's other parent is consistently violating the court's orders regarding custody and visitation, you may want to bring both a motion to enforce litigant's rights and a motion requesting a change in the parenting arrangements. An attorney can help you decide which motion or motions would be necessary and appropriate.

Penalties for Interference

In cases involving failure to comply with parenting orders, New Jersey family law judges have authority to order whatever remedies are justified under the particular circumstances of an individual situation. In an appropriate case a court might order temporary or permanent changes in the parenting plan, including some or all of the following, taken from New Jersey Court Rule 5:3-7:

- compensatory parenting time for the parent who has lost time,
- changes in transportation arrangements for visitation,
- changes in the children's pick-up location, or
- a change in the primary residential parent.

A court can also impose additional penalties, including ordering the interfering parent to:

- pay the other parent's attorney's fees and court costs,
- attend parenting classes or counseling,
- pay for counseling for the children or for the other parent,
- pay any costs resulting from non-compliance with court orders,
- participate in community service, or
- comply with a warrant for arrest.

Interfering with court-ordered parenting time is serious and can even be a crime in New Jersey. A parent who conceals a child from the other parent for the purpose of interfering with custody or visitation may have to serve jail time.

Defenses to Interference

If you are attempting to escape from the other parent's imminent violence, or if you believe that your child is in imminent danger from the other parent, you may have a defense to charges of interference, but you must contact DCP&P (1 (855) INFO DCF.), the local police, or the district attorney's office in your child's county of primary residence and reveal the child's location as soon as possible (and always within 24 hours). A parent fleeing from domestic violence can also bring a custody action in an appropriate court as soon as reasonably possible.

If you believe that your situation entitles you to a defense against charges of interference with custody or visitation, do not risk making yourself vulnerable to such charges; contact an attorney or DCP&P to ensure that you are complying with the law. The contact information for DCP&P is included in the "Resources" section at the end of this chapter.

Parents who are not receiving timely child support payments are not entitled to block visitation by the non-paying parent, but must instead address their concern in a legally appropriate manner such as by filing a motion with the court. Child support and parenting time are two entirely independent matters.

Practical Tip: Never withhold child support for the other parent's failure to allow you visitation.
Child support is not something that you pay in exchange for visitation rights. On the contrary, the purpose of child support is to cover expenses for your children when they are with the other parent rather than with you. If the other parent is denying your visitation rights, your legal remedy is to file a motion in court to enforce those rights.

FAQ: What can I do if my child's other parent refuses to spend court-ordered time with the children?
If your children's other parent consistently fails to exercise visitation rights—or if that parent has primary residential custody but continually leaves the children with you for much longer than your court-ordered visitation time—you can ask the court to modify your parenting time schedule based on a substantial change in circumstances. You may also have a case for modification of your child support order.

Termination of Parental Rights

The involuntary termination of parental rights requires a separate court action, called a family guardianship case. Parental termination hearings are specifically addressed in N.J.S.A. 30:4C-15-15.2, available on-line from the New Jersey Legislature.

DCP&P usually initiates these actions, although another party can also file a case after providing notice to DCP&P. With limited exceptions, the law requires DCP&P to file a guardianship case immediately whenever any one of five specific conditions is present, or in any case where a child has been in an out-of-home placement for 15 out of the most recent 22 months. The exceptions include cases in which a child is living with a relative who can care for the child permanently, cases in which DCP&P shows that termination of parental rights is not currently in the child's best interest, and cases in which DCP&P has not yet given the parent adequate help as required by law. Once DCP&P has filed a guardianship petition, the law requires the court to hear the case within 3 months.

The primary objective of DCP&P is family reunification. Before filing a case for termination of parental rights, the agency must employ reasonable efforts to help parents remedy conditions preventing them from caring for their children. How much effort is reasonable will vary from case to case, but in most cases, efforts must include working with the parent to develop a plan for appropriate services, providing agreed upon services, keeping the parents informed of the child's progress, and facilitating appropriate visitation between parent and child.

If DCP&P is unable to locate a parent, the agency can begin a termination case based on abandonment. In most cases, for a court to find that a parent has abandoned a child, it must find that despite being able to do so the parent has not contacted the child, the child's foster parent, or DCP&P for at least six months, and DCP&P has been unable to locate the parent after reasonable efforts. If it is not possible to determine either parent's identity—for example, if an infant is found unattended—and DCP&P has exhausted all reasonable methods of identifying the parents, termination may begin without delay.

Grounds for Termination

For a court to terminate parental rights, DCP&P must prove one of the following five grounds by clear and convincing evidence:

- the parent or parents, guardian, or other person having custody and control of a child has been convicted of abuse, abandonment, neglect of or cruelty to the child;
- the child is currently in the care or custody of DCP&P and the best interests of the child require placement under guardianship, because:
- the child's safety, health, or development has been or will be seriously impaired by the parenting relationship,
- the parents are unable or unwilling to eliminate the harm, and delay in permanent placement will add to the harm,
- DCP&P has thoroughly investigated and exhausted potential alternatives to terminating parental rights and has made reasonable efforts to help the parents cure the problems that led to the child's removal from the home, and:

- termination of parental rights will not do more harm than good;
- the parent or guardian has failed for one year following the child's removal from the home to remedy the circumstances leading to the removal, despite being physically and financially capable of doing so and despite having received reasonable assistance;
- the parent has abandoned the child; or
- the parent has committed, attempted, or planned to commit, a serious crime such as murder or aggravated manslaughter, or has committed a serious act that resulted or could have resulted, in the death of or significant bodily injury to the child or another child of the parent.

Placement with Potential Adoptive Parents:

Termination of parental rights is an extreme step and requires a high level of proof that a child's needs require termination. While protecting a legal parent's constitutional rights is a major concern, an even greater concern is avoiding serious physical or emotional harm to a child. Children who are placed with appropriate alternate caregivers usually develop emotional bonds with those caregivers over time, creating the potential for a second trauma if a child must be removed from a successful out-of-home placement.

For this reason, courts have decided that in a case where a child has become emotionally bonded to a temporary caretaker who is willing to adopt the child, the continuing harm that would result from a delay in placement can include the psychological harm that would be likely to result from the child being removed from the custody of the temporary caretaker.

If the parental rights of both parents are terminated, the result will generally be that DCP&P becomes the guardian of the child for all purposes, including placing the child for adoption.

Legal Representation:

Legal representation is critical in a case involving termination of parental rights. If you are a parent or legal guardian, and your child has been removed from your custody by DCP&P, you should hire an attorney. If you cannot afford to hire an attorney, The New Jersey Public Defender's Office of Parental Representation (OPR) may be able to provide an attorney for you. Children will always receive a separate court-appointed attorney.

An experienced New Jersey family law attorney can provide additional information regarding the legal process and the rights of both parent and child in this type of case.

New Jersey Kinship Legal Guardian Law

New Jersey law also provides an option called a "kinship legal guardianship," which in some cases will allow a court to appoint a permanent guardian for a child without terminating the rights of the legal parents. Anyone who is caring for a child in New Jersey can apply for kinship legal guardianship provided that certain criteria are satisfied. If a child is the subject of a current DCP&P court case, the application must be made through DCP&P. The child's parents can also request the court to consider appointing a particular person as a kinship legal guardian. The New Jersey Kinship Legal Guardianship Law can be found in N.J.S.A. 30:4C-84-91, also available on-line from the New Jersey Legislature.

The appointment of a kinship legal guardian transfers most parental rights to the guardian. While a parent may occasionally be able to regain custody after appointment of a kinship legal guardian, in most cases the arrangement will be permanent in order to prevent further disruption to the child's stability. While this makes appointment of a kinship legal guardian a serious step for a parent, it can be the best option for parents who are unable to care for children and who may otherwise be facing complete termination of parental rights.

A proposed guardian who meets the basic requirements will have to undergo a home assessment and a criminal background check before approval.

Requirements for Application
- the proposed guardian has cared for the child for at least 12 months,

- the biological parents of the child cannot care for the child and are unlikely to be able to care for the child in the foreseeable future,
- the proposed guardian is a relative of the child or is a family friend,
- the proposed guardian is financially able to care for the child, and
- it is in the child's best interest to remain in the care of the proposed guardian.

Rights of the Kinship Legal Guardian

The kinship legal guardian assumes most rights and responsibilities of a legal parent, including:

- making decisions regarding the child's care and well-being,
- consenting to routine and emergency medical and mental health care,
- developing and consenting to the child's educational plans,
- helping the child apply for admission to college,
- ensuring the child's safety, and
- ensuring the child's overall maintenance and protection.

Rights of the Legal Parents

After a court has appointed a caregiver as a kinship legal guardian, the legal parents lose their rights to custody, but retain the following rights and responsibilities:

- visitation with the child,
- payment of child support,

- power of consent over the child's legal adoption, and
- power of consent over the child's legal name change.

Termination of the Guardianship

A kinship legal guardianship normally lasts until a child turns 18. A parent who wishes to terminate a guardianship sooner will have to prove by clear and convincing evidence not only that the parent can now care for the child, but also that it is in the child's best interests to have custody returned to the parent. Courts prefer not to disrupt a kinship legal guardianship as long as the guardian is maintaining a stable home for a child.

Kinship Navigator Program

The New Jersey Department of Human Services, Division of Family Development, operates a program called the Kinship Navigator Program (211) located at the official State of New Jersey website: http://bit.ly/njkinship which provides information, referrals and follow-up services to grandparents and other relatives caring for children. Caregivers and parents can also obtain additional information about kinship legal guardianship from an experienced family law attorney.

Chapter 9

Child Custody Case Studies

In the following case studies all of the parties' names have been changed to protect the privacy of the families.

Case Studies:

1. Shared Legal & Physical Custody
2. Developing a Parenting Plan for an Infant

1. Shared Legal & Physical Custody:

The following case demonstrates how challenging it can be to work out a child custody arrangement that not only fits within each parent's schedule, but also adequately addresses the age-appropriate needs of children. It also shows how courts making decisions about child custody in divorce look closely at how a couple has shared parenting time during marriage:

Jim and Kelly were married for five years before they made the difficult decision to divorce. At that time, they had two children, Ella, age three and Charlie, age one. Both before and since Ella's birth, Jim and Kelly have each pursued full-time careers and have both been actively involved in the hands-on care of their children. Both children attend full-time day care, including before and after care to allow sufficient time for Jim and Kelly to commute back and forth from their New Jersey home to their demanding jobs in New York City.

During their marriage, Jim and Kelly worked together to establish a routine that allowed them to meet their children's needs while also working to develop their individual careers. They typically dropped the children off at day care together in the morning and also picked them up together on the way home. On weekdays they divided child care responsibilities as equally as possible. In the mornings, Kelly got Charlie and Ella dressed and ready for day care while Jim packed lunches and snacks and readied the diaper bag and backpacks. In the evenings, Kelly fed the children dinner and Jim was in charge of baths, teeth brushing and pajamas. Both parents took turns reading the children bedtime stories. They also took turns staying home if a child was sick and could not go to day care or needed to go to a doctor's appointment. Weekends were family time, spent mostly together.

In spite of this very equal and successful parenting arrangement, Kelly believed that having one primary custodial parent and one primary home after the divorce would provide the children with greater consistency. She proposed that Charlie and Ella live with her during the week and spend only alternate weekends with Jim. Jim was unhappy with this idea. After being so involved with his children on a day-to-day basis, he was not willing to change his role to that of a weekend dad. He proposed that the parents instead alternate full weeks, so that the children would spend one week at a time at Kelly's home and one week at a time at his home.

Because Kelly and Jim were not able to reach an agreement that both of them were satisfied with, an expert forensic psychologist performed a "best interests" custody evaluation. The psychologist concluded that neither Kelly's nor Jim's proposal adequately addressed the current best interests of Ella and Charlie. Kelly's proposal would deprive them of the day-to-day care they were accustomed to getting from their father, while Jim's position would take both parents away from the children for periods that were too long to be developmentally appropriate. Ella and Charlie were both still very young and the psychologist believed that they would have the best chance of continuing to form and maintain strong attachment bonds with each parent if they were able to see each of them on a regular basis without long stretches of time in between.

The evaluator recommended a shared parenting schedule with more frequent transitions, consisting of Mondays and Tuesdays with Kelly, Wednesdays and Thursdays with Jim, and alternate three-day weekends (Friday through Sunday) with each parent. The court agreed with the evaluator that this schedule would provide the children with greater consistency and stability than an alternating weekly schedule, while also giving each parent enough time with the children to maintain an integral role in caring for them on a day-to-day basis.

2. Developing a Parenting Plan for an Infant

The following case demonstrates how a plan can be worked out that addresses the developmental needs of a newborn and provides for adaptation over time:

Kyle, age 27, and Jenna, age 33, were together as a couple for only a few months before Jenna became pregnant unexpectedly. Jenna had always wanted children and even though the relationship with Kyle did not last, she decided to keep the baby. She found out it was going to be a boy and named him Sam.

At first Kyle was shocked to learn about the baby and tried to talk Jenna out of continuing with the pregnancy. Eventually though, he told her that he wanted to participate fully as a father and support his child. Jenna was not sure she was happy about this. She felt that Kyle was immature and irresponsible and that she would just as soon have him out of her life. She contacted a family law attorney to help her determine what the right thing to do would be. The attorney explained that New Jersey law recognized that it was generally best for children to have two involved parents. She gave Jenna some sample parenting plans, and Jenna began to feel better about the idea that Sam would have a father in his life.

Kyle and Jenna talked extensively about each of their schedules. Jenna also shared with Kyle everything that she had learned about infant bonding and what kind of schedule would be good for the baby. Eventually Jenna and Kyle decided to pursue the following plan:

After Sam was born, Kyle would visit with him for three to five hours at a time, three times a week, spaced throughout the week. Kyle agreed to take a parenting class and learn CPR to calm Jenna's fears about leaving him with the baby.

After about 6 months, Kyle would extend one of the visitation periods to about eight hours, and when Sam was between 9 months and a year old, Kyle would start to have one overnight visit per week, with the other two weekly visits extended to 6 hours each.

If this went well, once Sam was between 1 ½ to two years old, Kyle would be able to spend at least one weekend per month with him, while also keeping the other visitation periods.

Kyle and Jenna agreed not to plan things out any further than this, but to do their best to co-parent cooperatively to meet Sam's needs as he continued to grow.

Further Information and Resources:

- For an overview of child custody issues in New Jersey, see New Jersey Child Custody, Visitation, and Parenting Time, located at the Weinberger Divorce & Family Law Group website: http://bit.ly/nj-child-custody.

- For an article providing valuable insight into the effect of divorce on children and the many benefits of New Jersey's "Kids Count" program, see "Can Kids Count on Us?" by Bari Z. Weinberger, located at the Weinberger Divorce & Family Law Group website: http://bit.ly/kids-count.

- For an article discussing New Jersey court decisions addressing the complex topic of burden of proof in relocation cases, see "Burden of Proof in Removal Cases: Who Has It – What Is It?" by the Honorable Herbert S. Glickman and Bari Z. Weinberger. This is located at the Weinberger Divorce & Family Law Group website: http://bit.ly/child-relocation.

- The New Jersey Department of Children & Families has a webpage containing excerpts from several New Jersey laws pertaining to child abuse. This is located at their official website: http://bit.ly/nj-dcf. The New Jersey child abuse laws are in N.J.S.A. Title 9.

- The Office of Parental Representation (OPR) is a unit of the New Jersey Office of the Public Defender. You can find additional information on their official website: http://bit.ly/parent-rep, or by calling the Administration and Management Office at (609) 341-3832. OPR has several regional offices located throughout the state.

- The National Center for Missing & Exploited Children maintains resources for parents and others relating to various aspects of child safety. You can visit their Missing Kids website at: http://bit.ly/center-missing or contact them by phone at (703) 224-2150 FREE. You can perform a quick search for a missing child on the website and you can report a missing child, or a possible sighting of a missing child, by calling their 24 hour hotline: 1 (800) THE-LOST.

For More Information

At Weinberger Divorce & Family Law Group all of our attorneys are engaged full time in the practice of family law. We are committed to providing honest recommendations and keeping the best interests of our clients and their children at the forefront at all times. Our attorneys will strive to resolve your matter out of court and will explore your settlement options, including New Jersey divorce mediation if appropriate in your case. When it is time to fight, we will do so vigorously to protect your rights.

You can find out more about our dedicated family law attorneys on our website, which is located at: www.WeinbergerLawGroup.com. Weinberger Divorce & Family Law Group offers an initial consultation with an experienced New Jersey Family Law Attorney at no cost.

Weinberger Divorce & Family Law Group has several office locations throughout New Jersey.

Weinberger Divorce & Family Law Group Headquarter Offices:
119 Cherry Hill Road, Suite 120
Parsippany, NJ 07054
Morris County

Tel: (888) 888-0919

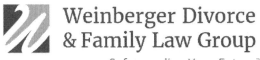
Weinberger Divorce & Family Law Group
Safeguarding Your Future™

Other Book Titles:
Weinberger Law Group Library Series
Of Family Law Guides

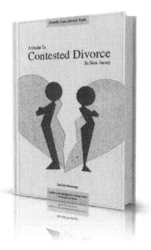

Contested Divorce

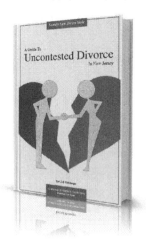

Uncontested Divorce

Child Support

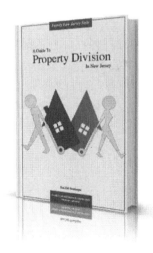

Property Division

Alimony

Print books and ebook versions of the Weinberger Law Group Library series can be ordered via Amazon or by visiting www.WeinbergerLawGroup.com